It's Your Money... What Am I Doing With It?: A Broker's View On Investing

It's Your Money... What Am I Doing With It?: A Broker's View On Investing

Kerry Scafella Haines

ISBN 978-1-257-96294-5

To Frank, who provides sage advice on form and structure,
To Jeanne, who plays the Hammerstein to my Rodgers,
To Kristen, who embodies strength and courage,
And to Mikey and Chrissy, who embrace each day with joy
and remind me to do the same.

ACKNOWLEDGMENTS

I would like to extend my deepest gratitude and appreciation to my clients. Without your questioning minds this book would not have been written. I hope that I have and will continue to answer your questions in a timely and useful manner. You have driven me to read more, learn more, and know more about the financial markets than I would have without you. I am a better, wiser person and hopefully you are the wealthier for it.

I would also like to thank Marie, owner of Red Door Studio, for her beautiful photography, and Keith Campbell, graphic artist, for his cover design. I am very lucky to know two such wonderful, talented individuals!

Disillusioned. After sixteen years, I am disillusioned with the industry to which I've devoted my professional career. I am disillusioned with the systems in place to execute the daily trades by which I ply my trade, and I am disillusioned with the regulatory agencies in place to police those systems.

Graydon Carter, editor of Vanity Fair, states it best: "Also to be counted on: if you hear something being blamed on a "rogue" element, you can be sure there is nothing rogue about it…'Rogue traders' on Wall Street periodically take companies for a ride, but they are only part of an industry that is itself now largely corrupt to the core."[1]

I admit that I am naïve in many ways. I believe in the basic decency and goodness of people, I try to give everyone the benefit of the doubt. But at this point, I must admit, my opinion of the people in this industry has dramatically shifted. As of this writing, another case of insider trading has just made the headlines. Raj Rajaratnam, founder of the Galleon Group, was found guilty on fourteen counts of insider trading and conspiracy. As written in the Wall Street Journal: "Still, no one would dispute that insider trading fuels the perception among investors that the game is rigged. They either play knowing the score—or shun investing."[2]

For most of us, the choice to invest or not to invest is a moot point. We have to have some place to put our money. We squash our doubts and discontents, tell ourselves that the financial systems in place are the only ones available, and pray that we won't lose our assets. As a broker, I pray that I won't give bad advice. I am consumed with the daily task of monitoring my clients' investments to make sure that no substantial amount of principal is lost.

In a perfect world, all brokers would feel this commitment. I would hope that the majority of brokers do feel it. However, I have known quite a few brokers in my career for whom the "get" is much

---

[1] Carter, Graydon (2011, June). Arts of Darkness, Acts of Courage. *Vanity Fair,* 46.

[2] Weidner, D. (2011, May 12). The Galleon Verdict: From Easy Money to Hard Time. The Wall Street Journal. Retrieved May 12, 2011, from http://www.wsj.com

more important than the result. As soon as a client is signed up and his assets are invested, he is put in the "gotten" file. If he is lucky he will warrant a once-a-year portfolio review meeting. If he is extra lucky he may get invited to an annual client appreciation event. Think about it—did you receive better treatment as a prospect than you do as a client?

I am reminded of a joke I heard many years ago about this situation. Mr. Smith dies and finds himself standing in front of an angel with an open book. The angel says, "Mr. Smith, it looks as though you've done some good things in your life but you've also done some bad things. I'm not sure whether to send you to heaven or to hell. So I'll make you this offer: you will spend one week in both places. At the end of the two weeks you can decide where you want to spend eternity." Mr. Smith thinks this sounds like a good plan, so he agrees to the angel's offer.

"The first week you will spend in hell," says the angel. The angel waves his arm and Mr. Smith finds himself descending on an escalator. He looks down and sees the most beautiful golf course he's ever seen, and on every green stands beautiful women holding trays of his favorite cocktail and food. He spends the week happily playing golf, drinking, eating, and fraternizing with the women.

At the end of the week he is back before the angel. "Now you will go to heaven," the angel says. He waves his arm and Mr. Smith ascends to a cloud where he finds that he has a harp and has grown a set of wings. He spends the second week floating in the clouds, playing the harp, and thinking deep thoughts.

Once again Mr. Smith finds himself before the angel. The angel asks, "You have spent a week in both heaven and hell. In which do you want to spend eternity?" Without a thought Mr. Smith replies enthusiastically, "Are you kidding? I want to go to hell! The golf, the food, the women—what could be better?"

Instantly Mr. Smith finds himself again descending on the escalator. But instead of a golf course, he sees fire and devastated wasteland. Flames consume him, and hideous beasts are whipping him with whips and chains. "But this isn't what I chose!" Screams Mr. Smith. "What happened to the golf course and the beautiful women?" From high above him Mr. Smith heard the angel's response, "Ah, Mr. Smith, last week you were a prospect, now you're a client."

It is not only with the treatment of clients that I take issue. It is with the hybridized, convoluted investments that are being created by

Wall Street. It is the fact that investors are being sold these investments without explanation or concern, and that the investors are purchasing them.

Perhaps the system is too big to change. Perhaps we have gone past the point of, as individuals, being able to effect substantive change in the way investments are produced or marketed. But then again, perhaps not. We can demand better service from our brokers. We can demand more information about the structure and content of investments. And we can demand more transparency in the pricing of these investments. Finally, we can exercise our right to say no, we don't want to own investments we don't understand.

I am not against capitalism, nor am I against investment for the mutual benefit of both broker and client. I am, however, part of the resistance to the shove of the major firms to sell a one-size-fits-all portfolio concept to the investor, the resistance to the belief that, if the firm creates the investment and tells us it's good for the client, then it must be good for the client. And finally, the resistance that if it benefits me, then it doesn't matter if it benefits you.

I recently realized that different clients through the years have addressed the same questions or areas of concern to me. This book contains my responses to the ten most salient of these points. The following pages are a collection of my observations and opinions formed over my years in the financial services industry. It is not my intent to malign a specific firm or individual, but rather to inform the investing public of the reasons, processes, and costs of the investments and services that they purchase.

After reading this book it is my hope that, should you be currently working with an investment advisor who seems to have the attitude "right or wrong, I'm still your broker," you will sever this relationship and find one much more to your financial benefit and liking.

I welcome any questions, comments, or insights that this book might inspire. You may contact me at Kerry@imyourbroker.net.

CONTENTS

CHAPTER 1

DON'T BELIEVE YOURSELF TO BE SEPARATE FROM THE MARKETS

The stock market is nothing more than a reflection of our consumption as individuals, and of a nation as a whole. It is not an entity entirely removed from daily life, but rather a gauge of where we are choosing to spend our money.

Each of us makes spending choices on a daily basis: we choose to buy coffee at the local coffee shop, we shop for groceries, we put gas in our cars, we decide to go out to a restaurant for dinner, we pay our mortgage or rent bills, we pay our utility bills, we purchase clothing and shoes, and so on. Over time, most of us start to make these choices subconsciously, but if we were asked to name any or all of our daily choices, we would realize that we are each supporters of specific companies.

If there is a product, an eating establishment, a utility company, or any other service of which you are a regular consumer, and it is a publically traded company, why wouldn't you choose to own stock in that company? Better yet, if that company pays a dividend to its shareholders, then you would not only be an owner of a company whose product you support, you would be paying yourself a dividend as well to be its supporter.

On the flip side, you could choose to loan money to a company you support by purchasing bonds issued by that company. You would then become a creditor of that company and would be helping them to operate by providing necessary capital while receiving an interest payment on that loan.

Sounds simple, doesn't it? It is. And yet we try to make it difficult. We don't believe that it could be that simple to make money. There has to be a trick or a smarter way of investing. How many times have you purchased stock in a company you support, made a nice return on it, but sold it because your head was turned by a "hot" biotech or .com company that was promoted as the next big thing? Perhaps you were given a tip by a cabdriver, or you overheard a couple of guys talking at a bar, or you received a call from your broker. And against your better judgment, before you really stopped to consider the situation, your greed instinct took over and you jumped.

Sometimes these tips work out, ninety percent of the time they don't. Warren Buffet is perhaps the best example of a "buy-and-hold" investor. And he is considered one of the smartest and most successful investors of all time. Here are two examples of investments in stocks of recognizable companies that were definitely buy-and -hold success stories.

In 1999, I was planning a series of seminars and was looking for some interesting stock information to include in my lecture. I happened across what is to me still one of the most amazing stock statistics I have ever read: if, in 1965, you were given the option to purchase one share of stock in any publically traded company, hold that stock and reinvest dividends all the way through 1998, and told it would outperform anything and everything in the investment universe, what company would you select?

Most people guessed IBM, General Electric, or Microsoft. But the answer is Phillip Morris. One share of Phillip Morris purchased in 1965, held through 1998 with dividends reinvested, including stock splits, became 5,565 shares. This gain from 1970 and beyond is shown in the chart below. Also illustrated are every dividend paid and every stock split. I have selected the Dow Jones Industrial average as an index for comparison purposes. The top line represents Phillip Morris (MO); the bottom line represents the DJIA. You can clearly see the difference in gain in just one stock of Phillip Morris over an entire index over the same period.

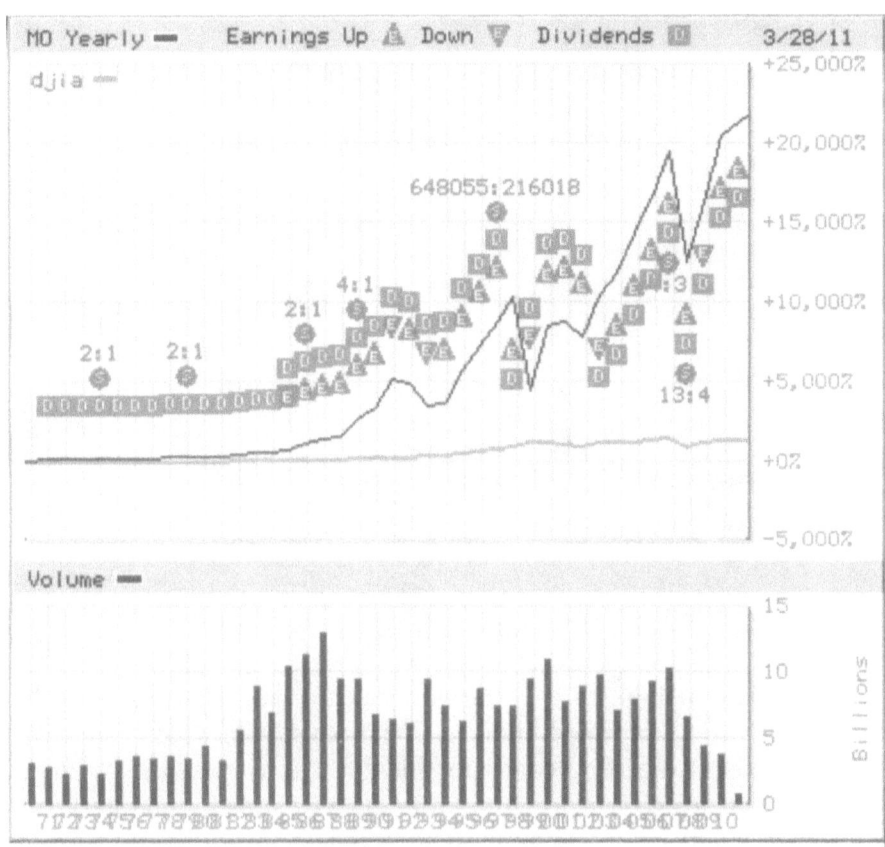

Chart of Phillip Morris stock 1970-2011.
www.altria.com

"But that was thirteen years ago!" you might be thinking. What could possibly repeat that same performance over the last ten years since 2001? Apple. The chart below shows the return of Apple stock from 2001 through the present. I have selected the Nasdaq Composite average for comparison, as many people have chosen to invest in index funds rather than individual stocks. The top line represents Apple (AAPL), with an over 3,000% return, while the bottom line represents the Nasdaq Composite, which appears relatively flat in comparison.

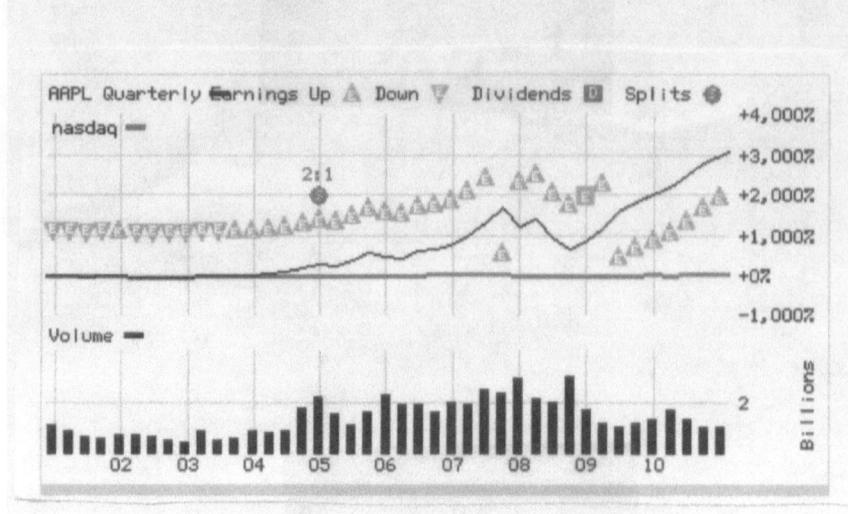

Chart of Apple stock 2001-2011
www.apple.com

It's easy to look in the rearview mirror and choose stocks that significantly outperformed indices. Who knew ten years ago what stock to choose? The first computer I learned to use was the Apple IIe in 1984. I then chose to own a series of Macintosh computers, and ultimately the large iMac desktop on which I am currently writing. I have always believed that the Windows operating system was a watered-down version of the iMac operating system, and that the iMac was much more user-friendly.

In 1998, when Apple was trading around eleven dollars per share, I had one client who was extremely interested in the company and who purchased 1,000 shares. Remember, this was the year Microsoft, Intel, Cisco, and Lucent were all going through the roof. But he wanted Apple. He has held those original shares over the last thirteen years, and has sold some periodically to purchase a Harley Davidson, a boat, and to pay off his mortgage. He still has enough to continue financing his life for a good number of years in the future. This is the ultimate example of buying stock in a company you understand and support even if it's currently out of favor with the rest of the investing public.

But you, the investor, are not solely to blame for poor judgment or hasty action. The financial services industry plays a huge part in this scenario. There is nothing more reviled by this industry than "dead" money. That is, money that is sitting in an investment on which no fees are being paid.

I firmly believe that it is this concept of dead money that has placed us in the position of thinking that the financial markets and instruments therein are so complex that we couldn't possibly understand them or choose investments for ourselves. It is this confusion over structure that allows us to view ourselves as separate from the markets.

A purchase of stock used to be a straightforward transaction. You purchased your shares, received a stock certificate for those shares, and placed the certificate in a safety deposit box. Usually those shares would stay there until there was a compelling reason to sell, such as a major purchase or the death of the shareholder. I have had quite a few clients past the age of ninety who held onto stacks of stock certificates in this manner. As they remembered the Great Depression, they didn't fully trust having all of their holdings in one place.

At some point, the financial services industry realized that by providing the convenience of accounts in which you could hold your stock certificates and your cash assets, they could remove the need for a trip to the bank to collect the certificates. Then, it became much easier to convince you that you needed to trade those stocks for something better. Plus, they could charge a commission on the sale and purchase of new stocks.

This concept also quickly changed. The need for revenue to fund the industry grew and new products were created. Among those new products were option contracts, mutual funds, structured investments, and derivatives. The greater the number of offerings from the financial services industry, the greater the opportunity for disassociation to be felt.

Information overload is another path to the road of disassociation. The introduction and proliferation of stock television channels, investment magazines, and online stock research sites has to be considered a positive development in our lives. But, the sometimes conflicting information that is provided by them is anything but positive. It is also important to remember that many of these sources, Money Magazine for example, are in the business to sell magazines— not investments. Notice that you will never see the same "hot" mutual fund on the cover from month to month.

It is very easy to access one or more of these resources to provide research on a company in whose stock you have interest. But what do you do if the television analyst advises a buy, the magazine article advises a hold, the online site is neutral, and your broker advises a sell?

This is the time that I ask you to remember the original reason you had interest in the company, especially if that company makes a product that you regularly purchase. Remember your belief in the product, and stand by your conviction to own stock in the company. It just might be a very smart purchase indeed.

I recently had an investment experience just like this. In January 2008, I was on vacation in Maui. I had been doing a lot of walking, and was very unhappy with my shoes. I stopped into a shoe store and saw a very nice pair of thong sandals that looked extremely comfortable. I tried them on, was immensely pleased with the fit and totally shocked at how incredibly comfortable they felt on my feet. It was like walking on pillows. I was even more shocked to discover that they were manufactured by Crocs.

I had never owned a pair of Crocs before this purchase. Quite frankly, I never cared for the clogs, and wasn't aware that the company produced any other style of shoe. I was however very familiar with the history of their stock. It had reached a peak price of $70.67 a share in 2007, then started a slow decline that turned into a rapid decline, and bottomed in late 2008 at $1.43 a share. This is illustrated in the stock chart below. The shaded line represents Crocs (CROX); the solid line is the DJIA.

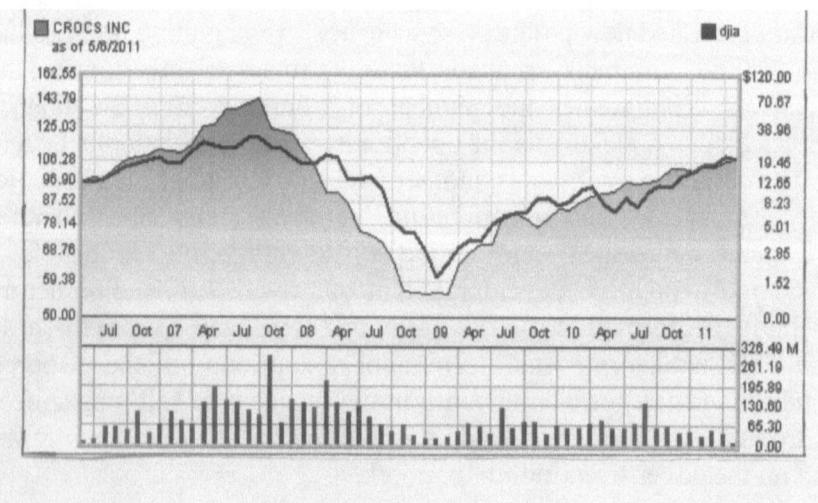

Chart of Crocs stock 2006-2011
www.crocs.com

At the end of 2008, I purchased another pair of Crocs thong sandals, then another pair in 2009. It occurred to me one day that I should follow my own advice and purchase stock in the company in whose shoes I was living! I bought shares for my clients and myself in January 2010 at $7.33 per share. Needless to say, the company at the time was not on the most favored list of any analyst. In fact, I think the majority of the analysts who covered the stock had an "avoid" or "sell" rating on it. I am happy to report that we now have a 195% gain in our investment, as the stock is trading today at $22.68 and yes, I am wearing my Crocs as I write.

If you love a product and buy it, there have to be other supporters of it as well. Don't believe that you are alone in your conviction, or that this belief and support does not tie you to the market in a significant way.

CHAPTER 2

NEVER OWN AN INVESTMENT YOU DON'T UNDERSTAND OR CAN'T EXPLAIN

The first question you should ask yourself prior to purchasing any investment is what am I buying? This question should be followed by, what does this company make or do? You should also ask what an option contract is. What is the structure of this investment? Is my principal at risk? Will I be earning a dividend? What is the yield? The bottom line is, you can never ask too many questions when you are about to make an investment purchase. It is the lack of questioning that has led many investors down the wrong path.

It is not always obvious what a company makes or does. As an investor, it is imperative to know what a company makes or does. The late nineties provide a great example of this with the proliferation of initial .com public offerings. Everyone wanted a piece of any new internet company that went public, believing that is was the next million-dollar idea. The brokers with whom I worked constantly told stories about advising their clients to buy huge quantities of these companies about which they knew nothing. Not one of them could explain what the companies actually did. Yet they were more than happy to urge clients to buy, and clients were more than happy to buy.

A related story: I clearly remember sitting in my sophomore English class in high school when the teacher asked the student next to me to define the word obsequious. She responded, "I know what it means, but I can't explain it," to which the teacher responded, "Then, no, you don't know what it means." If you can't define it, you shouldn't own it.

All brokers have access to analysis provided by many sources, their own firm, Standard & Poor's, whatever system is used to provide quotes, and others. There is never a reason for a broker to neglect to provide you with information about a company in which he wants you to invest. There should also never be a reason why, as an investor, you wouldn't want to read that information.

It is far too easy to use the blame game for our own laziness or lack of interest in research. You might say, "But that's why I hired a broker—to do the research for me." As a broker, I understand and fully embrace that responsibility. However, not all brokers do. You are the first and best line of defense when it comes to protecting your own assets. Never assume that an investment about which you know nothing is right for you, just because someone tells you it is, and don't assume that your broker knows it's right for you just because he says it is. Make him prove it.

OPTIONS

Option contracts can be an extremely effective way of hedging your investments. However, I never recommend the use of these to any client who does not understand what they represent. An option contract represents the right, but not the obligation, to buy or sell a specific amount of a given stock, commodity, currency, index, or debt at a specified price during a specified period. Options are very complex and require a great deal of attention and maintenance. If I have numerous engagements and plan to be away from my stock monitor for any extended period, I will not purchase option contracts for a client. If you are unable to maintain contact with your broker, you should not purchase them, either.

The most common use for option contracts in basic investing is to provide downside protection on a large individual stock holding through the writing of covered call contracts. This strategy can potentially save you from a loss due to market volatility. If your broker recommends this strategy to you, make sure he thoroughly explains the process and provides you with the total dollar amount to be gained by selling the contracts, the cost (commission) of selling the contracts, and the exact potential percentage gain or loss of the strategy.

Please, also remember that employing a covered call writing strategy in volatile markets can produce a large number of short-term gains if the underlying stock is called. If you have tax issues or are not looking to pay the higher tax on short-term gains, this is probably not the best strategy for you.

STRUCTURED INVESTMENTS

The next investments to examine are those called structured investments. Structured investments are either principal-protected or principal-at-risk investments, with equity index-linked performance. They can be based on equity securities, indices, interest rates, currencies, or commodities.

The U.S. Securities and Exchange Commission (SEC) defines these in the following manner: "securities whose cash flow characteristics depend upon one or more indices or that have embedded forwards or options or securities where an investor's investment return and the issuer's payment obligations are contingent on, or highly sensitive to, changes in the value of underlying assets, indices, interest rates, or cash flows."[3] What? There are so many variables to protection and performance with these instruments that I believe the only reason they were created was to make money for those who issue them or those who sell them—*not* for those who invest in them. I view these investments like a trip to Vegas when you choose to bet against the house.

A friend recently told me that he had been advised to purchase one of these investments. His broker explained to him that if the underlying assets outperformed the index to which it was linked he would receive a specific return. But if it underperformed, he would get back what was left of his original principle. His question to his broker was: "It sounds to me as though the house is placing the bet, and I'm in a position to bet against the house. Why would I do that?" Exactly. Why would you do that?

Structured investments are generally recommended to provide diversification for clients with larger portfolios, the rationale being that these clients have the assets to sustain larger losses without complaint. I believe that sufficient diversification can be achieved in a more simple way through the use of investments that are easy to understand. If, however, you would rather roll the dice with a structured investment because a 22,000% gain in Phillip Morris just isn't sexy enough for you, then so be it. You've been warned.

---

[3] Securities and Exchange Commission. (2005, June 15). Report And Recommendations Pursuant to Section 401(c) of the Sarbanes-Oxley Act of 2002 on Arrangements with Off-Balance Sheet Implications, Special Purpose Entities, and Transparency of Filings By Issuers. Retrieved April 17, 2011 from http://www.sec.gov

CDOS AND ASSET-BACKED BONDS

Two recent articles in the Wall Street Journal are of particular concern to me. The first article, "Subprime Bonds Are Back", described the comeback in subprime bonds, CDOs (collateralized debt obligations)[4]. The second article, "Asset-Backed Bonds Go Exotic", illustrated the growing demand for exotic asset-backed bonds[5]. Neither of these investments are something I would ever own or recommend, but their resurgence is worth examining for another reason.

Subprime bonds, as you may recall, are the instruments that caused the beginning of the global financial meltdown of 2008. These are bonds that are constructed of groups of subprime mortgages, considered the riskiest mortgages due to their high levels of nonpayment and defaults. The mortgages are packaged into an investment similar to a bond, and are set to pay a certain interest rate. However, if any of the underlying mortgages go into default, the interest rate is immediately affected, and the principal may also be at risk. Even though the underlying mortgages in the bonds were held by homeowners with the lowest credit ratings, the bonds were routinely given AAA ratings by both Moody's and Standard and Poor's, the major rating agencies in this country.

In his book *The Big Short,* author Michael Lewis clearly illustrates that the rating agencies did not thoroughly examine these investments. The firms who were packaging, promoting, and selling the bonds didn't examine or understand them, either. If the people creating them couldn't explain them, what chance would there be for the investor to understand them?

At the time of the crisis there were millions of these bonds in the system, representing billions of dollars of investment. There were many holders of these bonds, including both institutions and individual investors. In fact, many banks and brokerage firms actively encouraged brokers to sell these bonds to their clients, as the firms were involved in the creation of the bonds and stood to derive additional revenue from the sales. I recall receiving daily emails about the availability of the CDOs with hyperlinks to take me directly to the inventory of them for sale.

---

[4] Wirz, M. & Ng, S. (2001, April 1). Subprime Bonds Are Back. *The Wall Street Journal.* Retrieved April 1, 2011 from http://www.wsj.com
[5] Shrivastava, A. (2011, April 4). Asset-Backed Bonds Go Exotic. *The Wall Street Journal.* Retrieved April 4, 2011 from http://www.wsj.com

The SEC has been investigating the major banks involved in the creation of the CDOs. Alleged misconduct by these banks includes overpricing of the mortgage-bond deals and the failure to disclose to the investors that hedge funds were actively betting on a fall in the housing market but were involved in the selection of the subprime mortgages that constituted the bonds.[6]

AIG, the giant insurance firm that was deemed "too-big-to-fail" by the government, had a huge portfolio of these CDOs that were purchased by the Federal Reserve during the bailout to save the company. AIG recently offered to buy back a pool of these bonds at fifty cents on the dollar. The Federal Reserve did not accept this offer because they believed that more money could be made by selling the bonds to other investors—including major insurance companies.

The fact that hedge funds have interest in these bonds now does not surprise me. The fact that individual investors have interest does. Why would anyone be willing to overlook the extreme damage to the financial system and the huge loss of capital caused by these investments? Is this risk worth a little more interest than is being earned on a traditional bond? Obviously, some believe it is. I do not, and I forewarn anyone who being is told to purchase these bonds to proceed with caution.

The increased demand for exotic asset-backed bonds is very surprising because the overall size of the market for these bonds is decreasing. Asset-backed bonds were traditionally composed of student, auto, and credit-card loans. Timber harvests, timeshare revenue, and cell phone-tower leases back the new class of these bonds. These new issues pay a higher yield, but also contain inherently higher risk.

Why are investors so willing to ignore the fact that the Federal Reserve created TALF (Term Asset-Backed Securities Loan Facility) in 2009 to support this market after its decline caused by the financial crisis? And if this market failed once, what is to prevent it from failing again? What is different this time?

ANNUITY CONTRACTS

Another area of concern is the purchase of annuity contracts. Annuities are wonderful investment tools when used for the right

---

[6] Fitzpatrick, D. & Eaglesham, J. (2011, April 4). Wachovia Targeted Over Sale of CDOs. The Wall Street Journal. Retrieved April 4, 2011 from http://www.wsj.com

reasons in the right circumstances. Each contract with each insurance company has specific riders, guarantees, and benefits that can vary greatly. Each rider, guarantee, and benefit has a cost. Therefore, it is imperative to completely understand what you are purchasing prior to signing a contract. Make note of the duration of the contract, and the duration of the guarantees.

You have probably heard that you should never own an annuity contract within an individual retirement account. I beg to differ. If the annuity has a guaranteed income or withdrawal benefit, you are not purchasing the annuity contract to provide tax deferral, but rather to provide a guarantee on your investments and your future retirement income stream. In this way, you are creating your own pension. You have effectively negated the possible dire consequences of a significant drop in the markets immediately prior to your planned retirement date.

If you were lucky enough to have purchased an annuity contract with a guaranteed living benefit issued in the period from 1997-2003, please don't ever be convinced to sell it or exchange it for another policy. The benefits and riders of these policies were so good that they are no longer available because the insurance companies that issued them can no longer buy the "reinsurance," or backup insurance, necessary to insure the guarantee. Several firms offered this living benefit, among them Transamerica, Equitable, and Ohio National. This benefit provided either the greater of market performance or a 5% or 6% guaranteed, compounded interest on your principal from the first day of investment, which would then be provided to you as an income stream when you decide to start drawing it.

In addition, these contracts provided the greater of either market growth or a 5% to 6% guaranteed, compounded interest on the death benefit from the first day of investment. With the performance of the market since 2008, I would bet that the guaranteed death benefit rider is significantly higher than the actual market value of the current death benefit. If you exchange this policy, you forgo this benefit and effectively cheat your beneficiaries out of a large amount of money. Don't do it!

LIFE INSURANCE

Life insurance is available in many forms. The four varieties of basic life insurance are: term life, whole life, variable life, and universal life. But the question you must ask first is: do you need life insurance?

I have had several clients who were single or widowed, who had no beneficiaries, and yet had been sold life insurance contracts by other brokers. If there's no one to be cared for, if there's no income to replace, no mortgage to be paid, then why buy life insurance?

There are always unique situations with individual investors based on the size of the estate. Perhaps the individual wants to leave his assets to a charitable organization, or wants to create a scholarship at his alma mater, or even wants to establish a foundation as his legacy. Life insurance trusts are used in many of these cases.

If you are an investor with sizeable assets who needs estate planning then, by all means, explore the world of insurance with both an estate planning attorney and an insurance specialist. If you do not have the assets that require this specialized service then do not feel compelled to purchase a life insurance policy.

Any or all of the above-referenced investments may have a legitimate place in your portfolio. I am simply recommending that you take the time to research and understand. Don't assume that the person recommending the product to you is more interested in your long-term financial health than in making the sale.

CHAPTER 3

It may seem like an obvious statement, yet you would be amazed at the number of people with whom I speak who haven't spoken to their broker in over a year, or who only receive a yearly courtesy call. Unfortunately, as the broker's need to gather assets in order to remain viable and compete effectively in the industry increases, the concept of customer service has decreased.

Over the years, I have known many brokers who sat at their desk reading a newspaper or talking to a fellow broker while allowing their phone to ring unanswered. They must believe that it makes them seem more important or busier if an assistant answers the phone.

Many brokers have tried to balance this situation by forming teams with other brokers and by adding customer assistants. While this may be an effective action for the broker, it still denies you, the investor, contact with the person with whom you have placed your investments and trust. For an investor, this is an unacceptable situation. If you place a call to your broker and do not receive a return call from him but from his "team" or a staff member, then I highly suggest that you rethink the relationship. No one is that busy. This should tell you that you are not in the top tier of clients. Doesn't call, doesn't care. Enough said.

CHAPTER 4

DON'T BELIEVE THAT BIGGER MEANS BETTER

The misconception that bigger is better applies to institutions, mutual funds, and even brokers. What happens when institutions become so large they are beyond the scope of law and regulation? The practices of the institution become the law. It is their way or the highway, take it or leave it. The concept of choice that we believe is always available to us becomes just that: a concept, not a reality.

This is the problem confronting the financial services industry today. Ten years ago, there were a number of smaller independent brokerage firms and regional banks. The largest banks in the country acquired some of these firms when some failed. Why does this matter? The larger the institution, the more support staff is needed to run operations for the institution, the more managers are employed to supervise the support staff, the more pressure is put on brokers to produce revenues to fund the operations, the higher and more numerous are the fees which are passed on to you, the consumer.

Have you received a financial transaction confirmation lately? If so, check it for a five dollar "service charge," in addition to any commission you paid. This began to appear several years ago. It was added to every transaction as a method to generate additional revenue for the firms to pay the overhead, similar to the fees charged on ATM transactions. This is purely a fee-generating item. The size of your transaction doesn't matter, nor does the frequency. Why are they able to charge this fee? Because it is an industry-accepted practice, and with the industry now consisting of four major financial services firms, to whom can you complain?

As anyone who has ever worked outside his home knows, each workplace has its own personality. Generally, the smaller the office, the more relaxed and congenial is the atmosphere in the office. The individual employee has a much greater chance of autonomy and recognition in this situation, as well as job satisfaction. In a service industry such as a brokerage firm, this translates into improved customer service and more personal service. It is not surprising that year after year, the smaller, regional brokerage firms receive higher satisfaction ratings from their investors than do their larger counterparts. Bigger does not equal better when measuring client satisfaction.

Now, examine a huge corporation with 270,000+ employees in multiple locations across the country and around the globe. The local individual offices might be small, but they all report to the one corporation. The home office dictates the whole atmosphere of the local branch. The atmosphere is not the only thing that suffers in this scenario. The ability to perform simple tasks such as asking an operational question becomes an exercise in both patience and endurance.

Recently, I had a procedural question to ask for a client. I was told to call an operations call center in another state for the answer. I called, and was given an answer by the first person with whom I spoke. The answer did not sound accurate to me, so I called back and received a different answer by another person. Just to check its accuracy, I called a third time and was given yet another answer by a third person. I strongly suspect that I could have called ten more times, spoken to ten other people, and received ten other answers. This would be hilarious if it were a one-time occurrence, or if it were not a client's money that was in question.

It seems that the sheer size of the corporation makes it impossible to have all employees on the same page, regardless of their job function. It would also stand to reason that this same size issue would make it difficult, if not impossible, for the governmental regulatory agencies to maintain a thorough oversight of these corporations.

If you are a client of a major brokerage, I strongly recommend that you closely monitor your investment account statements just as you would your bank statements and other financial statements. I have several clients who tell me that they don't open the statements when they arrive (you know who you are), especially when the market was down the previous month. I also recommend finding an internal advocate within the branch to assist you with any issues that might arise. This should be your broker, but if he isn't willing to perform that service for you (too busy answering his phone), then one of his assistants will suffice.

This same issue of size affects the mutual fund industry as well. Historically, the larger a mutual fund is in terms of assets, the lower the performance that fund returns. This is true regardless of the sector in which the fund invests, although numerous empirical studies show that small-cap, illiquid stock funds tend to suffer more than their large-cap, more liquid counterparts. There is a simple reason for this. It is a very different thing to sell five million shares of a stock than to sell five thousand shares of a stock. A mutual fund manager of a large international stock fund in the nineties once likened this size of stock sale to making a sharp left turn in the Titanic. Most mutual fund managers set an asset limit for themselves when they start a new fund and, once they reach it, close the fund to new investors.

It is only common sense to know that when a broker has too many clients he can't do a quality job for each one. He must either place all the clients in the same type of investment to monitor it effectively, or go the route described in Chapter 3 by building a team and farming smaller clients out to other brokers. If you are one of the top ten clients in terms of asset size, this won't matter to you. To everyone else, it should. There is simply no way to respect the individual needs of each client, and further to abide by the "know your customer" rule mandated by the Bank Secrecy Act and the USA Patriot Act, if you're dealing with too many clients.

Unfortunately, the ever-shrinking percentage of commissions paid to the broker and the ever-increasing percentage of commissions paid to the firms makes this growth of client base mandatory. It is impossible to survive in this industry if you are not constantly bringing in new assets. I always compare our job to sharks—we keep swimming or we die. This significant push to grow bigger and bigger continues to increase on an annual basis.

This focus on asset gathering rather than asset managing is not good for the client who expects professional management of, and attention paid to, his investment portfolio. There is simply not enough time in the day. This focus has spurred the extreme growth in fee-based products, outside money managers, wrap programs, etc., which I discuss in later chapters.

It would stand to reason that the biggest brokers, measured by their number of clients, are not necessarily the best money managers, but the better marketers. They have effectively worked within the systems to warehouse assets with outside managers and in fee-based accounts, which frees them to concentrate on the acquisition of new clients.

It would also stand to reason that these same brokers would have much less personal knowledge of their clients, and would be much less able to be proactive rather than reactive in their management of these clients' assets. In a steady, upward-moving market, perhaps this isn't such an issue. But in the volatile markets that we've been experiencing for the last three years, it's become a huge issue.

A discussion of the potential downfalls of size would not be complete without a mention of Bernie Madoff and the largest Ponzi scheme in history. Bernie Madoff was allowed to perpetrate his scheme unchecked for over twenty years. There were, I am sure, many who looked at his practices but very few who chose to see what was actually happening. One individual not only saw, he attempted to alert the proper authorities. His name is Henry Markopolis, and his incredible story of complete refusal to listen by the SEC can be read in his book *No One Would Listen*:

"Tens of thousands of lives have been changed forever because of the SEC's failure. Countless people who relied on that agency for the promised protection have lost more than can ever be recovered. In some cases people lost everything they owned. And truthfully, the SEC didn't even need to conduct an extensive investigation. My team had given them everything they needed."[7]

This is a clear indictment of the SEC, a very large institution, for its failure to regulate or to even acknowledge wrongdoing on the part of Bernie Madoff. It is also an example of the willingness of people to follow the crowd without question. Madoff's operation was big and successful, therefore it must be good. My neighbors trust him, so should I? If we learn nothing else from this debacle, it should be to carefully screen and monitor our advisors, and not to feel influenced by the size of his office or the size of his client base.

---

[7] Markopolis, H. (2010) *No One Would Listen.* Hoboken, NJ: John Wiley & Sons, Inc. 8

CHAPTER 5

WHAT YOUR BROKER DOESN'T KNOW *CAN* HURT YOU

Perhaps the biggest disappointment in my career in the financial services industry occurred just after my initial training. I had just completed all of my securities licensing and three-month internship before I went to a month-long training program, eager to learn everything I could about investments. I quickly realized that I was not there to learn about investments, but to learn how to sell investments. I may as well have been selling refrigerators. The only prerequisite of trainees entering the financial services industry, I learned, was a bachelor's degree, in any field.

Because I had two bad personal experiences with brokers who, through poor investments and inattention lost substantial sums of my money, I made it my mission to learn as much as I could about any investment product I planned to recommend to my clients. Unfortunately, all brokers do not share my desire for knowledge. I have known quite a few brokers who believe that money management is not their job, money acquisition is, so why should they bother to learn about investments? They fashion themselves to be "financial quarterbacks," the guy who has a handful of experts to whom he can throw your question. He may not know the answer, but hey, he can get you to someone who does.

While it is good to have experts in specific fields to whom you can address questions—estate-planning attorneys and accountants, for example—it is not good to have a broker who lacks basic knowledge of investments, the economy, or current world events. These are the individuals who don't think it necessary to read the *Wall Street Journal*, *Barron's,* or any other trade publication. They find it perfectly acceptable to simply regurgitate any information published on their company's website, and studiously avoid forming an opinion of their own lest they be questioned about it.

The investor can be damaged by lack of broker knowledge in many areas. The two areas in which I've observed the biggest lack of knowledge are fixed income investments and a lack of personal knowledge of the investor.

Following the financial crisis of 2008, there has been much speculation over the safety of certain fixed income investments. As I mentioned in Chapter 2, the re-emergence of CDOs and asset-backed bonds should be a huge concern to the investing public. Of equal concern, however, should be the large number of fixed income exchange-traded funds (ETFs) that employ leverage as a means to maintain a stated dividend.

Leverage is used as a means of increasing the potential return of an investment. However, leverage magnifies both gains *and* losses. It is for this reason that the broker must not only be aware that leverage is being used, he must be aware of the ratio of leverage—2:1, 3:1, etc.—and the type of financial derivatives or debt that constitute the leverage. Firms have gotten much stricter in allowing these types of investments into clients' portfolios. Most require that the client choose "speculation" as the main objective for the account. However, I suspect that most clients check this option without fully understanding the potential risks involved in this type of investment.

All funds that employ leverage must state this in their prospectus, as well as the ratio and type of leverage. I understand that most people look at a prospectus as instant "circular file" material. Your broker should not. Ask the questions. Understand the investment prior to its purchase.

Municipal bonds have gotten an extreme beating in the press of late. Since analyst Meredith Whitney came out with her dire prediction of catastrophic defaults in the municipal bond markets, many investors have been concerned for the safety of their bond holdings.

I strongly disagree with Ms. Whitney's prediction, and now advise my clients to maintain, and, in some cases, to increase their municipal bond holdings. Municipalities are allowed to declare bankruptcy if their home states allow it, even if the states themselves are not. However, most brokers, and most clients for that matter, are unaware that there are twenty-five states in this country that do not have a state statute that specifically allows municipalities to declare Chapter 9. In these states, the municipalities would need to petition the state for authorization to declare Chapter 9, making the process much more difficult.

It is for this reason that an AAA-rated general obligation municipal bond issued by a municipality in Virginia (a state that does not allow Chapter 9) would be more desirable than the same rated bond issued by a municipality in Alabama. It is also true that while Chapter 9 is a bankruptcy filing, the debts of a municipality are not wiped away as they are for an individual or a corporation, but rather restructured to allow the municipal more time to repay. This restructuring may include reduction of the outstanding debt or interest rate, refinancing of the debts, or extension of the original bonds.

If you have significant municipal bond holdings, and have never had this discussion about Chapter 9 with your broker, please do so. Demand that he list the twenty-five states for you that do not allow Chapter 9 filings. If he can't answer, send me an email. I will answer. If you are concerned about the safety of your municipal bond holdings, you might also ask that he explain why you hold bonds in the other twenty states if they are not your home state.

There is a section on the standard new account information form used by brokerage firms called "investment objectives." When you open an account, you are supposed to choose from one of several options—conservative, moderate, moderately aggressive, and aggressive—to define the basic purpose of the account, and therefore the types of investments that would be suitable for the account. For example, you would not be able to purchase leveraged ETFs in an account coded as conservative. As these are extremely generic terms, it is up to the broker to fully interview, define, and understand the client and his investment objective rather than relying on description alone.

It has been my experience that the investment objective that an individual chooses may not accurately reflect his investment purpose, or even his true level of risk tolerance. I have had clients tell me they have a moderate risk tolerance level, only to realize that any investment other than a CD would prevent them from sleeping at night. The only way for a broker to learn these things is to spend the time getting to know the individual. This simply cannot be accomplished in a one-hour meeting.

It is imperative, for both the financial and emotional health of the client, that the broker spends whatever time is necessary to define objectives as completely as possible. The process of investing is not one of stasis, but of fluidity. The changing life circumstances of the client should be reflected in his portfolio. Lack of time spent with or lack of knowledge of the client can cause irreparable damage.

CHAPTER 6

DON'T ASSUME ASSET ALLOCATION IS THE ONLY ANSWER

Have you heard anyone say recently, "Asset allocation worked before—didn't it?" Asset allocation is defined as an investment strategy that aims to balance risk and reward by apportioning a portfolio's assets according to an individual's goals, risk tolerance, and time horizon. The three main asset classes—equities, fixed income, and cash and equivalents—have different levels of risk, so each will behave differently over time.

Prior to 2008, this theory was largely successful on its own. If one asset class significantly underperformed, another would usually outperform, thereby maintaining balance in a portfolio. The financial crisis devastated all asset classes across the board. It didn't matter if you were holding equities or fixed income, or any combination of the two, your portfolio significantly shrank in size. In addition, your cash holdings went from earning a respectable level of interest to around .25%, a level at which the tax you paid on the interest was more than the interest earned. There was no place to hide.

The theory of asset allocation as the only investment process required is still being pushed on investors by the major firms by way of the asset allocation plans, or estate-planning programs, they promote. It evokes the "set it and forget it" concept: if your assets are properly allocated, you need not worry about daily or even quarterly global events. Each of the major firms has their own form of this plan. The main purpose of this plan is not solely to create an asset allocation model for the investor, but to uncover previously undisclosed assets. Some firms charge for these plans, some don't. And yes, brokers and their assistants can collect bonuses based on the number of these plans they are able execute for their clients.

The problem with this traditional mode of planning is that it neglects to calculate the current global economic situations and the advent of algorithmic trading, both of which may cause extreme moves in the markets on any given day and virtually nullify any attempt at balance through asset allocation alone. Now is not the time to rely on a computer-driven model, but on human attention to daily events.

We cannot rely on the fact that we operate in a global economy and count on the revenues derived by American companies from foreign countries, yet ignore the fact that there are serious economic issues with several of the major countries in Europe. To employ nothing but a buy and hold strategy, regardless of decline in certain sectors, is to invite devastation into a portfolio. If a sector declines by fifty percent, that loss must be made up prior to any gain being realized. And, there is no guarantee that the sector will recover in a timely manner.

The perfect examples of this are the financial services and banking industries. Due to their creation of, and complicity with, the subprime mortgage fiasco, the stocks of the companies in these industries were decimated. Prior to 2008, the stock of Bank of America was trading around fifty-five dollars per share. It dropped to less than five dollars per share in January 2009, but has only recovered to a price of $11.88 per share today. Another company with an equally substantial price decline was Citigroup. Their stock traded around forty dollars per share, dropped to around one dollar, bounced back to four dollars, and stopped. The company recently declared a ten-for-one reverse split to bring the share price back above forty dollars.

The financial services industry had always been considered a solid, conservative industry in which to invest. The companies paid nice dividends, and generally didn't have large price swings. If you were one of the investors who had a portion of your portfolio allocated to this industry, and your broker failed to recommend a sell prior to 2009, you lost eighty percent of your money. Two years later, you haven't even begun to recoup any of the lost principal, nor have you receive a dividend while waiting.

It is not enough to establish a plan, allocate assets accordingly, and leave it to fate. The plan must be constantly monitored and adjusted based on market conditions. No investor should feel compelled to invest in all asset classes because a program or plan dictates that he should.

CHAPTER 7

THERE IS NEVER A REASON TO "WRAP" A MUTUAL FUND

I will state this again. There is never a reason to wrap a mutual fund. A mutual fund wrap program is a type of managed account created by the financial services company to continually charge an annual management fee on assets invested in mutual funds. They provide many reasons to justify the need for additional "management" and thus, the fee. A few of these reasons are 1) increased awareness by the broker of potential fund manager changes within the funds, 2) access to no-load funds that would not be otherwise accessible through the standard brokerage account, and 3) the ability to move between fund families and trade funds with no additional sales charge.

I argue the following: 1) the fund manager information is readily available through Morningstar for which the investor does not need to pay an additional fee, 2) the no-load funds are not necessarily the great bargain you might think they are, and 3) mutual funds are meant as long-term investments, not trading vehicles.

Recently, I had an experience with a mutual fund trade that I would like to share. A client of mine had owned a mutual fund for several years and was unhappy with its performance. He called me to ask for my recommendation of a replacement fund. We discussed a couple of other funds and chose a new fund. I placed the trade and was immediately contacted by the operations department of my firm. They demanded to know why we exchanged the fund, whether or not the client was aware of the costs associated with purchasing a mutual fund in the first place, and if the client understood that a mutual fund should be considered a long-term investment.

I find it extremely ironic that, had this same client owned this fund in one of the firm's mutual fund "wrap" programs, we could have traded the fund five times and not been questioned. It seems as though mutual funds are only considered long-term investments by the firm if you are not paying them an additional "wrap" fee to own it.

I have always said that the person who created the concept of "no-load" is a marketing genius. The term no-load, to our brains, is the financial equivalent of fat-free. We hear those words and immediately think "this has to be good for me." All funds, even those that are no-load, charge fees. There are management fees, which include those to pay the fund's managers, non-management fees, which include administrative fees, transfer agent fees, board of directors fees, and custodian fees, 12b-1 fees, which include marketing and advertising fees, and trading costs, which are the actual costs of the trades made in the fund's portfolio.

Those mutual funds that offer a "front load" have generally reduced fees across the board because the bulk of the fee is paid when the fund is purchased. Those funds that offer a "back-end load" still have higher annual internal fees to compensate for the lack of up-front charges. The same higher annual internal fees apply to the "no-load" funds, as the lack of immediate payment of fees on the initial purchase has to be collected. Bottom line, the funds' managers and operating expenses have to be paid by someone, and this means you, the investor. All of the actual fee information for any fund is available in that fund's prospectus. Your broker should be aware of the costs of any fund he is recommending, and should be able to list them for you.

Why then, with the knowledge you now have about the internal costs structures of mutual funds, would you choose to pay an additional, unnecessary management fee on those funds?

CHAPTER 8

The following statement needs to be made before we delve into the differences between commission-based accounts and fee-based accounts: all brokers are paid commission only, not salary. Brokers receive anywhere from twenty-five to forty percent of the total commissions they generate based on their total annual production. It is within the broker's discretion to discount his portion of the commission charged, but never the portion that goes to the firm. We generally don't receive expense accounts or corporate credit cards, and are treated more as self-contractors even though we are W2 employees.

Prior to 1995, clients were charged a fee for most financial transactions. In 1995, the SEC released a statement that "fee-based accounts serve to better align the interests of the advisor with the interests of the investor." In 2005, this course was completely reversed. All the rules were restated as it was realized that rather than protecting clients from commissions charged for excessive transactions, it exposed them to paying a fee on assets that would otherwise be sitting in their accounts fee-free. Specific ratios for activity and non-activity were established. In the last six years, these ratios have become muddled—not, I believe, in the best interest of the client, but rather in the best interest of the firms to produce as much revenue as possible while avoiding potential arbitration. Simply put, if you make too many trades in a managed account you would generate more revenue for the firm through a commission-based account, but if you make too few trades you become a potential case for arbitration.

The average stock commission ranges anywhere from 1.5% to 2.5% based on the price of the stock and the total number of shares purchased. Remember, brokers have the ability to discount their percentage of the commission.

Let's pretend that you have $1,000,000 worth of investments in your portfolio. You have $400,000 in mutual funds, $450,000 in municipal bonds, and $150,000 in individual stocks. During the year, you decided to do five stock trades, each totaling around $30,000. If you were paying commissions on those trades, you would have paid around $2,250, which represents an average of 1.5%. However, if you were in a fee-based account, you would have paid $10,000 for those same trades, as you paid a fee based on the total assets in your account of one percent. Who made more money in this scenario?

I am reminded of the great phrase employed by Ron Popeil in his infomercial for the chicken rotisserie: "Just set it and forget it." Unfortunately, most brokers still have this mentality when recommending a fee-based account to clients. If your assets are happily producing annual fees for your broker, regardless of the market conditions, then he is free to go off and lure other clients into the same product. He can then see you once a year for an annual review, convince you to "let the portfolio cook," and move on to other things. He has fulfilled his minimum required fiduciary responsibility, and will continue to do so unless you question this process.

Fee-based accounts for equities make much more sense than such accounts for fixed income. I manage an equity portfolio on a fee basis in which I have placed clients who wish to have a slightly more aggressive trading strategy for a portion of their portfolios. I do not, however, place clients with municipal or corporate bond portfolios in fee-based accounts. To me, that would be like paying someone to watch the grass grow. There is simply no way to justify the expense on such a low turnover of investments.

I am not advocating one structure over the other. I have always based my recommendation on a client's comfort level and stated preference for either commission or fee. If you are an investor who likes to trade frequently, then you would generally pay far less to trade in a fee-based account. If, however, your portfolio resembles the one used in my above scenario, please calculate your actual potential transaction costs versus an annual fee prior to signing on the line. If you interview a broker who tells you he only manages fee-based accounts and this isn't the most cost effective solution for you, walk out and go to someone else. There are still plenty of brokers who are willing to work within your rules rather than the institutions by which they are employed. This is, after all, a service industry. Demand and expect quality service.

CHAPTER 9

A broker arranges transactions between a buyer and a seller and gets a commission when the deal is executed. A financial advisor provides financial services including investment advice and financial planning through the use of stocks, bonds, mutual funds, options, and insurance products. So, what's in a name?

It may seem like an argument over semantics, but I think it is a little more than that. When I started in the business there was no shame in being called a broker. After all, it represented what we did on a daily basis: find an investment, place a trade, and receive a commission. When the major firms decided that a portion of a client's assets were insufficient—they wanted it all—we were called financial advisors, I assume because this title implies a higher level of service. More bang for the buck, if you will. With the huge surge of assets flowing into outside managed money and fee-based accounts, the title financial advisor could be used to describe an individual who studied a client's portfolio, carefully considered the proper investments, then placed the assets into these investments.

However, if a financial advisor meets with a client, provides a list of money managers with whom he plans to place the client's assets, and does so, is he not acting as a broker? Several years ago, I asked the broker in the office next to mine a question about a stock I was considering buying. He said, "I don't know anything about stocks. I advise, I don't invest."

In a perfect world, all financial advisors perform the duties ascribed to them in the dictionary's definition of the title. In the real world, some do and some don't. Your job as an investor is to decide what services you need and what amount of compensation is reasonable for those services.

CHAPTER 10

WHY DO I NEED FINANCIAL ADVICE?

You need financial advice because you are human. And, as a human, you need the validation that only comes from an interaction with another human. You need someone with whom to discuss ideas, someone with whom to celebrate when times are good, and someone to blame when times are bad. You need to share the burden of your life circumstances and your financial decisions. Ultimately, if this is a positive relationship, your financial advisor will feel more like a good friend or even family member than someone who is looking at you as a number.

I am always interested in the reactions I receive when I tell people what I do for a living. Some people cringe and try to change the subject immediately as though afraid that I will ask them for their money. Others want to extol the virtues of their own financial advisor. Still others, the do-it-yourselfers, will tell me how well they have been doing managing their own portfolios, and then, without fail, will ask me for some stock recommendations. I believe I have gotten more requests for my stock picks from individuals who profess to be excellent stock pickers than from my own clients.

I would like to remind these individuals that it is for these ideas, for my intellectual product, that I am compensated. I deal with air. I produce nothing but intangibles. So do not presume that I or any other financial advisor should offer free advice as though it were normal cocktail conversation. If you really want my advice and respect my opinion, make an appointment, listen to my recommendations, and allow me to manage your portfolio. Otherwise, ask your buddies or that cab driver for advice, and continue to manage your own investments.

I consider myself very fortunate to know and advise my clients. They are an extremely diverse group of individuals who represent a wide spectrum of the population. Most have been working with me since early on in my advising career. We have been through some amazing times together, both in terms of world events and financial events. And as disillusioned as I find myself with the industry, it is for my clients that I continue to work within it on a daily basis. It is my sincere wish that your current advisor feels and demonstrates this same commitment to you.